Pebble® Plus

Habitats around the World

An Ocean of Animals

by Janine Scott

CAPSTONE PRESS
a capstone imprint

Pebble Plus is published by Capstone Press,
1710 Roe Crest Drive, North Mankato, Minnesota 56003.
www.capstonepub.com

 Books published by Capstone Press are manufactured with paper
containing at least 10 percent post-consumer waste.

Library of Congress Cataloging-in-Publication Data
Scott, Janine.
    An ocean of animals / by Janine Scott.
        p. cm. — (Pebble plus. Habitats around the world)
    Includes bibliographical references and index.
    Summary: "Color photos and simple text describe animals and their adaptations to the ocean"—Provided by publisher.
    ISBN 978-1-4296-6814-9 (library binding)
    ISBN 978-1-4296-7151-4 (paperback)
    1. Marine animals—Adaptation—Juvenile literature. I. Title. II. Series.

    QL122.2.S36 2012
    591.77—dc22   2011005314

Editorial Credits
Gillia Olson, editor; Lori Bye, designer; Svetlana Zhurkin, media researcher; Laura Manthe, production specialist

Photo Credits
Alamy/Phototake, 17
Digital Vision, 20 (top)
Dreamstime/Bashta, 13; Krzysztof Odziomek, 21; Vladimir Seliverstov, 20 (bottom)
Getty Images/Jeff Rotman, 18–19
Photodisc, cover, 6–7
Shutterstock/Kamira, 5; Rich Carey, 10–11; WDG Photo, 1; Willyam Bradberry, 9
Visuals Unlimited/David Wrobel, 14–15

Note to Parents and Teachers

The Habitats around the World series supports national science standards related to life science.
This book describes and illustrates animals that live in the ocean. The images support early
readers in understanding the text. The repetition of words and phrases helps early readers learn
new words. This book also introduces early readers to subject-specific vocabulary words, which
are defined in the Glossary section. Early readers may need assistance to read some words and to
use the Table of Contents, Glossary, Read More, Internet Sites, and Index sections of the book.

Printed in the United States of America in North Mankato, Minnesota.
072016   009865R

Table of Contents

Full of Life

Looking from shore, the ocean seems to hold just water. But it's bursting with animals! These animals live in different parts of the ocean, or zones.

Coastal Zone

The coastal zone is where land meets water. Coastal animals often live in and out of water. Crabs scuttle on the beach. Sea birds fly overhead.

Sunlight Zone

The sunlight zone is the top layer of the ocean. Most of the world's fish live in this zone. Small fish munch plants. Sharks eat the small fish.

Coral reefs grow in the sunlight zone in shallow water. Millions of animals live on each reef. Sea anemones spend their lives clinging to one piece of coral.

sea anemone

Mammals live in the sunlight zone too. Manatees graze on sea grass. Sea otters dive and play in seaweed. Giant blue whales swim in the open ocean.

Twilight Zone

The twilight zone starts about

660 feet (200 meters) deep.

It gets very little sunlight.

The dragonfish has lights

on its body to lure prey to it.

Dark Zone

The dark zone starts at about
3,300 feet (1,000 meters) deep.
It's very dark and very cold.
Tube worms cluster around
thermal vents to stay warm.

Unknown Life

More than half of Earth is
covered in very deep water.
Very little has been explored.
Who knows what animals
scientists will find in the future.

Fun Facts

〜〜 If a sea star's arm breaks off, it can grow another one.

〜〜 Animals like seals, beluga whales, and walruses live in the cold waters near the north and south poles. They all have a thick layer of fat, called blubber, to keep them warm.

The whale shark is the world's largest shark. It gets about 45 feet (14 meters) long.

Sea otters eat shellfish, such as clams. They smash the shells open by hitting them against a rock.

To scare away predators, the porcupine fish sucks in water. Its body fills up to appear twice its normal size. Its spines pop out too.

Glossary

coral reef—a type of land made up of the hardened skeletons of corals; corals are small, colorful sea creatures

explore—to go searching or looking around

graze—to eat grass or other plants

lure—to draw something near

mammal—a warm-blooded animal that has a backbone and feeds milk to its young; mammals also have hair or fur

sea anemone—a sea animal that has many tiny arms, called tentacles

shallow—not deep

thermal vent—a crack in the ocean floor that spews super hot water

Read More

Mason, Janeen. *Ocean Commotion: Life on the Reef.* Gretna, La.: Pelican Pub., 2010.

Salas, Laura Purdie. *Colors of the Ocean.* Colors All Around. Mankato, Minn.: Capstone Press, 2011.

Slade, Suzanne. *What If There Were No Sea Otters?: A Book about the Ocean Ecosystem.* Food Chain Reactions. Mankato, Minn.: Picture Window Books, 2011.

Internet Sites

FactHound offers a safe, fun way to find Internet sites related to this book. All of the sites on FactHound have been researched by our staff.

Here's all you do:

Visit *www.facthound.com*

Type in this code: 9781429668149

 **Super-cool stuff!** Check out projects, games and lots more at **www.capstonekids.com**

Index

Word Count: 214 (main text)
Grade: 1
Early-Intervention Level: 18